T0132235

Things My Grandmothers Said

by

Tracye Stormer

Illustrated by Kristen Munroe

AuthorHouse™
1663 Liberty Drive
Bloomington, IN 47403
www.authorhouse.com
Phone: 833-262-8899

This book is printed on acid-free paper.

This project is funded through a grant from the John & Susan Bennett Memorial Arts Fund of the Coastal Community Foundation of South Carolina and Sistah On A Budget Productions. Special thanks to Laura Carter.

Also by Tracye Stormer

The Three Graces

ISBN: 978-1-4343-3343-8 (sc)

Library of Congress Control Number: 2007907398

Print information available on the last page.

Published by AuthorHouse 01/29/2024

authorHOUSE®

In loving memory of Anna Belle Wilson,
Roberta Faulkner, Mattie Mackey and Marjorie Mitchell.

I have four grandmothers and I love them very much. I especially love to visit them and hear them talk about when they grew up. It's like I get my very own history lesson. My grandmothers say things to me that I sometimes don't understand.

My Grandma Ma Mitchell lives right in the Lowcountry of South Carolina with me. I get to see her every day. She has a day care center and she even kept me when I was little. All of the children love her.

They think she is their Grandma – but really she belongs to me. Sometimes I go by the day care to help her with the children. She always makes time to sit and talk to me.

One day I went by the house and Grandma Ma Mitchell was cooking a pot of her famous collard greens. They are the best! I think I could eat the whole pot if she let me. She makes good red rice, too. She always makes the red rice for the church fish fry.

When I went in the house I said, "Grandma, something sure smells good!"

She laughs and says to me "I can't keep the smell out of your nose but I can sure keep the taste out of your mouth."

I look at her and say, “Huh?”

She throws her head back and laughs at me. “Don’t be answering me with no huh.”

“Yes Ma’am”, I reply.

“Baby, I can’t stop you from smelling my good cooking but I can make sure you don’t taste it if I don’t give you any. So I can’t keep the smell out of your nose but I can sure keep the taste out of your mouth.”

I gave that some thought. “Okay Ma Mitchell, I get it.”

And you know what? Now I do.

I went by the day care after school one day and I was really sad. "Why is your face so long?" Grandma asked.

"Well, my friend Ericka is having a party on Saturday, and the church is having a picnic and now Jessica is having a party on Saturday too. I want to go to all of them!"

Ma Mitchell just shook her head and said, "You can't catch every hog."

I look at her and say, "Huh?"

"I'm not going to tell you again – don't you answer me with huh."

"Yes Ma'am", I reply.

"Baby, it means you can't do everything. Some things you just have to miss or let go. You can't catch every hog."

I gave that some thought. "Okay Ma Mitchell, I get it."

And you know what? Now I do.

I remember when I got mad at my Mother because she wouldn't buy me those red patent leather shoes from the store. They were shiny and sparkly just like the ones in the movies. I stomped around the house and stomped around the house. I heard Grandma Ma Mitchell laughing at me. That only made me madder.

Then I heard her say, "A cow will need his tail to fan a fly more than once."

I looked at her and said, "Ma'am?"

"Baby, you're gonna need your Momma again and again. Now you walking 'round here pouting over a pair of shoes and your Momma makes sure you always have everything you need. Even a cow needs his tail to fan a fly more than once – you're gonna need your Momma again. Learn to be grateful."

I gave that some thought. "Okay Ma Mitchell, I get it."

And you know what? Now I do.

Grandnana lives about three hours away in the city of Columbia. It's the capital of South Carolina. I get to see her regularly because sometimes we go and spend the weekend at her house. When I see Grandnana I just want to smile. She can make me laugh and laugh.

Lots of people love Grandnana and come by to see her. They act like she is their Grandmother - but really she belongs to me.

There is a big hill on the road to Grandnana's house and we ride our bikes up and down the hill. She is always telling us to watch out for cars coming and don't go too fast. We always yell 'okay' and keep right on riding and going fast.

One day a car was coming behind me on the hill and my bike started spinning from the gravel. I fell down hard and scraped both of my knees.

Grandnana was standing at the door saying, "Get up and come on in. You threw your candy in the sand."

I looked at her and said, “Huh?”

“Don’t be answering me with no huh.”

“Yes Ma’am”, I reply.

“Baby, you wanted to do your own thing now you have to come on in and just sit down. You had a good thing going and you didn’t want to listen. You threw your candy in the sand.”

I gave that some thought. “Okay Grandnana, I get it.”

And you know what? Now I do.

Sometimes I do things that make Grandnana mad. Like that time I popped her pearl necklace. Instead of telling her what happened I tried to hide it. I think that upset her more than anything because she always tells me things can be replaced. She didn't say that this time. As a matter of fact she didn't say anything. She went around the house doing her everyday stuff and she didn't say a thing to me. After tiptoeing around her all day I was ready to talk.

She looked at me and said, "I can have you in the roof of my mouth and my tongue won't even know you're there."

I looked at her and said, "Huh?"

"I'm not going to tell you again – don't you answer me with huh."

"Yes Ma'am", I reply.

"Baby, when you've done wrong say you've done wrong. Don't go around lying and trying to hide it. That's not good. Now I always tell you that things can be replaced. It's always best to tell the truth. I stopped talking because you can be around me and it won't bother me a bit. I can keep going like you're not even here. That's why I said you can be in the roof of my mouth and my tongue won't even know you're there."

I gave that some thought. "Okay Grandnana, I get it." And you know what? Now I do.

Grandnana always asks me about my friends. What kind of things do they do? Are they good or are they bad and always in trouble? I laugh and tell her I think my friends are good because they're my friends. Then she asks me what other people think about my friends. I told her I didn't know.

My grandmother looks at me and shakes her head. "People judge you by the company you keep. Birds of a feather flock together."

I look at her and say, "Ma'am?"

"Baby when you see people in a group it's because they have something in common. You don't see geese flying with bluebirds. Birds of a feather flock together. You will become just like the people you hang out with. Everybody watching from the outside will know what kind of person you are because of the people you surround yourself with. Be careful when you choose your friends."

I gave that some thought. "Okay Grandnana, I get it."
And you know what? Now I do.

My Grandma Mattie lives in the Upper State of South Carolina. She doesn't hold her tongue and she tells it like it is. I like to stand next to her because I'm taller than her. She always tells me that still don't make me grown. I get to visit her for a week during the summer.

She doesn't drive but she can get anybody to give her a ride. They love her like she belongs to them – but really she belongs to me.

Sometimes when we don't have a ride we catch the bus. We were riding the bus downtown when I told Ma Mattie that a lot of my friends were no longer on the dance team. We got a new teacher and she put some of them off the team.

"A new broom sweeps clean," she replied.

I looked at her and said, “Huh?”

“Don’t be answering me with no huh.”

“Yes Ma’am”, I reply.

“Baby, your friends were probably not following all the rules. They got away with stuff with your old teacher because she knew them. Your new teacher isn’t going to put up with too much foolishness – she’s cleaning house. A new broom sweeps clean.”

I gave that some thought. “Okay Ma Mattie, I get it.”

And you know what? Now I do.

I have chores even when I'm at my Grandmother's house. I have to sweep the porch and some nights I do the dishes and clean the kitchen. Sometimes I don't want to do it so I rush through it so I can go play or watch TV.

Grandma Mattie will call me and say, "Once a task is just begun never leave until it's done. Be the labor great or small, do it well or not at all."

I looked at her and said, "Huh?"

"I'm not going to tell you again – don't you answer me with huh."

"Yes Ma'am", I reply.

"Baby, when you 're given an assignment you always do your very best. Your work is a representation of you. It tells people how you think of yourself and how they should think of you. Always do your best. That's why I say once a task is begun you never leave until it's done. Be the labor great or small – do it well or not at all. And not at all is not an option."

I gave that some thought. "Okay Ma Mattie, I get it."

And you know what? Now I do.

I really wanted to go to science camp that summer. I was supposed to write a paper saying why I liked science. But I didn't do the paper and I didn't get to go to camp. I went to Grandma Mattie's house instead.

I told her, "My Momma wouldn't let me go to camp."

She said, "That's not the way I heard it, but every tub has to sit on its own bottom."

I looked at her and said, "Ma'am?"

"Baby, there comes a time in life when you have to be responsible for your own actions. Your Momma wanted you to go to camp but you didn't do what you were supposed to do. You have to learn to be responsible. Every tub has to sit on its own bottom."

I gave that some thought. "Okay Ma Mattie, I get it."

And you know what? Now I do.

My Grandmama Ro lives in the Upstate too. I get to spend a week with her in the summer and I always have my birthday at her house. She makes sure I have ice cream, cake and some presents.

There are always people coming to her house and they always leave with something in their hands. Everybody loves Grandmama Ro and they wish she belonged to them – but she doesn't. She belongs to me.

Grandmama Ro loves to eat fish. She would fry fish almost everyday. Everyone in the neighborhood comes by her house and she always makes them sit down and eat a little something with her while they talk.

When the ice cream man comes around the curve, she passes out quarters so all the children can get ice cream. I asked her why she is always giving stuff to people.

She looked at me and said, “A closed fist never lets anything out and nothing can ever get in.”

I looked at her and said, "Huh?"

"Don't be answering me with no huh."

"Yes Ma'am", I reply.

"Baby, you have to give in order to receive. You can't get anything if you aren't willing to share sometimes. Always be willing to share. A closed fist never lets anything out and nothing can ever get in."

I gave that some thought. "Okay Grandmama Ro, I get it."

And you know what? Now I do.

Sometimes the preacher would come by the house after church for Sunday dinner. You better act like you had some home training and not show out. You had to keep your elbows off the table, pass the food in a nice manner and you better not stuff your mouth with food like you haven't eaten in a week.

Grandmama Ro said, "You should be able to sit in the presence of princes and paupers."

I looked at her and said, "Huh?"
"I'm not going to tell you again – don't you answer me with huh."
"Yes Ma'am", I reply.
"Baby, you should have good manners at all times whether you're in the presence of the very rich or the very poor. Always put your best foot forward. You should be able to sit in the presence of princes and paupers."

I gave that some thought. "Okay Grandma Ro, I get it."
And you know what? Now I do.

One afternoon, I stormed into the house and slammed the door. Grandma Roe was in the kitchen. She walked into the living room and just looked at me.

“The kids outside won’t play with me!” I said.

“Well Baby, you’ll catch more flies with honey than vinegar.”

She turned and went back in the kitchen. I pouted for a moment and then I followed her.

I looked at her and said, "Ma'am?"

"Are you being nice so they will want to play with you? You can't be in charge all of the time. Be sweet and they will come to play with you. You'll catch more flies with honey than vinegar."

I gave that some thought. "Okay Grandma Ro, I get it."

And you know what? Now I do.

Now you know my Grandmothers and you see why I love them so much. I'm glad they belong to me but I don't mind sharing them with other people. That's why I shared them with you.

It's like your very own history lesson. Maybe you'll think about the things they said that I didn't understand and you can learn from them too.

Oh – one more thing.

My Grandmothers said, "You should learn some things just from living."

The longer we live the more we should learn.

Get it? I do.

About the Author

Tracye Faulkner Stormer is a native of Beaufort, South Carolina. She is the owner of Sistah On A Budget Productions (www.sistahonabudget.com) and author of the fiction novels *In the Pursuit of Happiness*, *Hooked Up* and the children's book *The Three Graces.* She is the mother of three wonderful children who encourage her writing dreams,

She holds a B.S. in Computer Science from Bennett College in Greensboro, North Carolina and an M. S. in Computer Science from Atlanta University in Atlanta, Georgia.

About the Illustrator

Kristen Munroe is a graduate of Auburn University and University of Georgia. A native of Atlanta, Georgia, she is a painter, sculptor and visual arts teacher, Kristen is also the illustrator of the children's book *The Three Graces.*

Printed in the United States
by Baker & Taylor Publisher Services